Concepts of Piano Theory

Level 5

Dear Teacher,

Concepts of Piano Theory provides a basic understanding of music, increases sight-reading abilities and prepares the student to analyze compositions at the earliest levels.

Each workbook introduces new terms and concepts that are reinforced with worksheets, practice exercises and composition analysis. Concepts learned in earlier levels are reviewed, tested and expanded upon in advancing levels. Answers to the **Level 5** tests, worksheets and exercises may be found in the **Concepts of Piano Theory, Teacher's Key**.

This workbook is made from recycled paper. By using products that are made from recycled materials, you are helping reduce landfills and recover renewable resources.

For a complete understanding of music, a thorough study of theory is necessary. **Concepts of Piano Theory** provides the information that should be understood by every advancing pianist.

TABLE OF CONTENTS

REVIEW OF LEVEL FOUR

1. Name all the sharps in order as they appear on the staff.
_____ _____ _____ _____ _____ _____ _____

2. Name all the flats in order as they appear on the staff.
_____ _____ _____ _____ _____ _____ _____

3. Write the name and Roman numeral of each degree of the Major Scale.
_____ ____, _____ ____, _____ ____,

_____ ____, _____ ____, _____ ____,

_____ ____

4. Write the names and Roman numerals of the three Primary triads.
_____ ____, _____ ____, _____ ____

5. Write the names and Roman numerals of the four secondary triads.
_____ ____, _____ ____, _____ ____,

_____ ____

6. Draw triads used in a Plagal Cadence in root position, 1st inversion, and
2nd inversion in the key of G Major. Label with Roman numerals.

Root Position   1st Inversion   2nd Inversion

7. Draw triads used in an Authentic Cadence in root position, 1st inversion,
and 2nd inversion in the key of B♭ Major. Label with Roman numerals.

Root Position   1st Inversion   2nd Inversion

8. List the four families of the symphony orchestra.
_____, _____, _____, _____

9. List two instruments from each family listed above.
_____ _____, _____ _____, _____ _____,

_____ _____

10. Draw the following ascending half-steps.

Chromatic   Diatonic   Chromatic   Diatonic

CPT 5

11. Draw the scale of D Major and its relative minor in natural form.
    Use Key Signatures.

    D Major   ___ minor

12. Draw the Major and harmonic minor scales below.
    Write the letter-names of the scales.

    ___ Major   ___ minor

13. Draw DOMINANT SEVENTH chords in root position and all inversions.
    Mark each inversion with a figured bass symbol. Use accidentals.

14. Name one composer for each of the four periods of music.
    _____, _____, _____, _____

15. Write the names of three early modes used in music.
    _____, _____, _____

16. Name the modal scale below.

    _____

17. How many phrases make up a period? _____

18. An antecedent phrase asks a question. Name the phrase that is the answer to the
    question. _____

19. Name the three sections of sonata-allegro form.

    _____   _____   _____

20. Circle the name given for A B A form.   Binary   Ternary

RELATIVE MINORS

For each one of the FIFTEEN MAJOR KEYS there is a minor key with the
same Key Signature.

Major and minor keys with the same Key Signature are called RELATIVE KEYS.
They are related by Key Signature but not by key-tone.

Review these two ways to locate relative Major and minor keys.

Find the sixth degree of any Major Scale. That will be the TONIC or KEY-TONE
of its relative minor.

On the keyboard play the MAJOR TONIC, count down three half-steps
(a minor third), and play the RELATIVE MINOR TONIC.

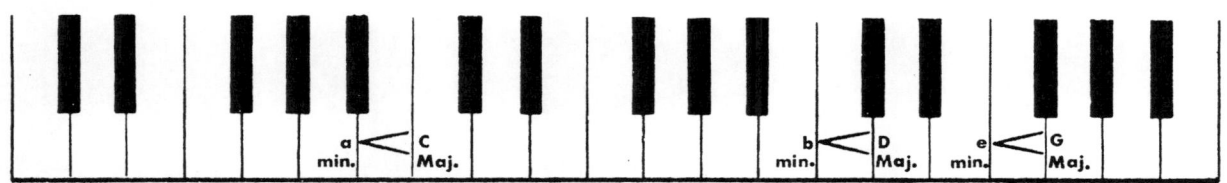

1. Draw the tonics for the following Major keys and their relative minors.
   Label M or m.

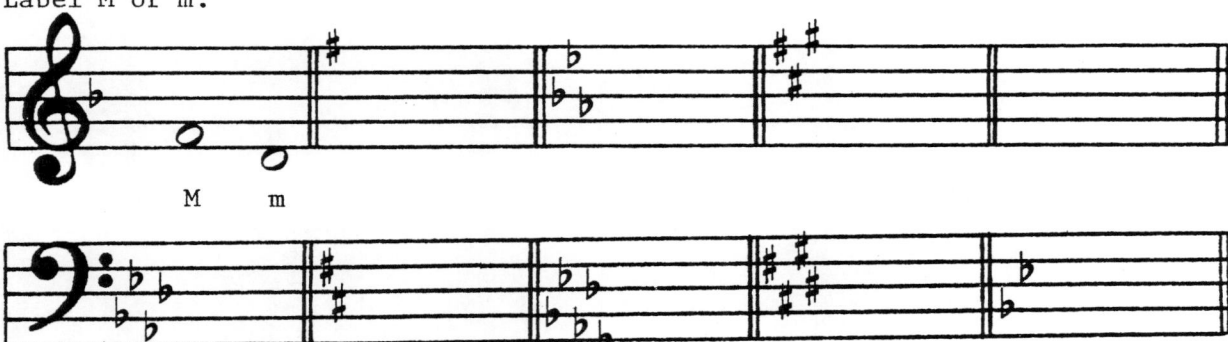

2. Draw the Key Signatures below. Label tonics M or m.

MINOR CIRCLE OF FIFTHS

The MINOR CIRCLE OF FIFTHS proceeds in the same way as the MAJOR CIRCLE.
The dominant of the scale becomes the next tonic on the circle.

Complete the Major and minor circle of fifths below. Place the letter-names for
the Major keys outside the circle and for the minor keys inside. REMEMBER THE
ENHARMONIC KEYS.

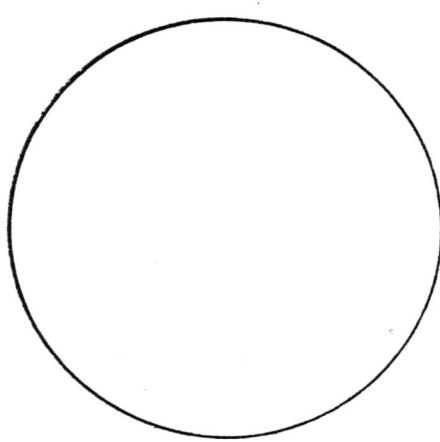

Draw the Key Signatures below. Draw the tonic Major and tonic minor triads for
each key. Label M or m.

| 2 flats | 6 flats | 3 sharps | 5 flats |

| 5 sharps | 4 flats | 1 sharp | 1 flat |

| 4 sharps | 3 flats | 2 sharps | 6 sharps |

MINOR SCALES

The MINOR SCALES are also diatonic scales with one note on each successive line and space. As in the Major Scales, the half-steps and whole steps are formed by the use of accidentals when needed.

MAJOR and MINOR SCALES with the same Key Signatures are called RELATIVES.

THE NATURAL (PURE) MINOR SCALE

The pattern of the NATURAL MINOR SCALE is: W - H - W - W - H - W - W

The half-steps fall between scale degrees 2 - 3 and 5 - 6.

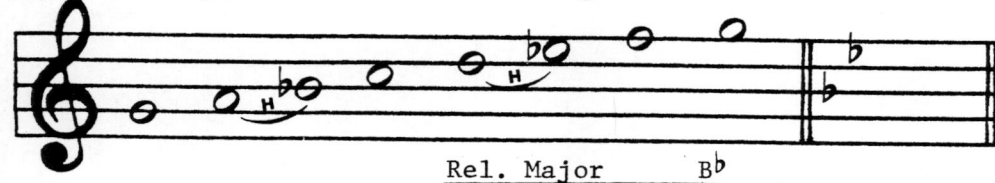

Rel. Major   B♭

Complete the natural minor scales below. Use accidentals. Mark the half-steps with slurs. Place the Key Signature after each scale. Write the name of the relative Major below each one.

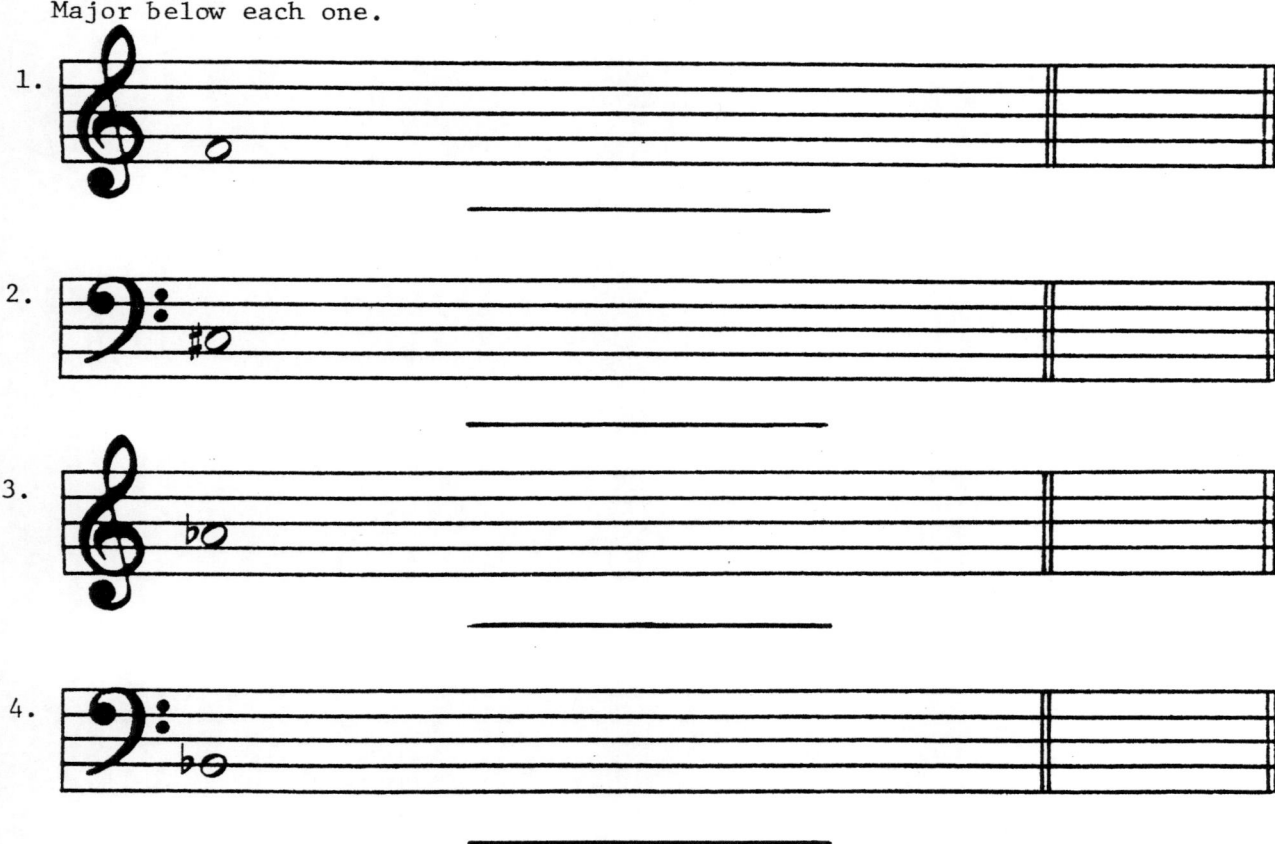

CPT 5

THE HARMONIC MINOR SCALE

The minor scale most often used in keyboard music is the HARMONIC MINOR.

This scale differs from the natural minor because the 7th degree of the scale is raised one half-step. Due to the raised 7th degree, there are three half-steps between degrees 6 and 7.

The pattern of the HARMONIC MINOR SCALE is: W - H - W - W - H - WH - H
(1½)

EXAMPLE   g natural minor   g harmonic minor

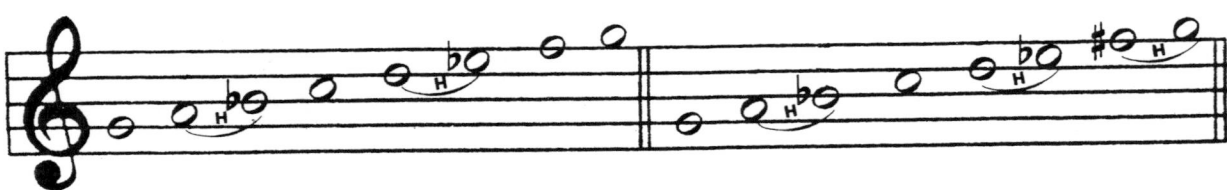

Because the 7th degree is raised a half-step, it is not unusual to find both sharps and flats in a harmonic minor scale.

Draw the harmonic minor scale on each key-tone. Use accidentals.

1.

2.

3.

4.

5.

6.

7.

8.

9.

10.

THE MELODIC MINOR SCALE

In the ascending MELODIC MINOR SCALE both the 6th and 7th degrees are raised one half-step each.. The descending MELODIC MINOR SCALE returns to the form of the NATURAL MINOR SCALE.

The pattern of the ascending MELODIC MINOR SCALE is: W – H – W – W – W – W – H

The pattern of the descending MELODIC MINOR SCALE is the same as that of the NATURAL MINOR.

G MELODIC MINOR SCALE (ascending)

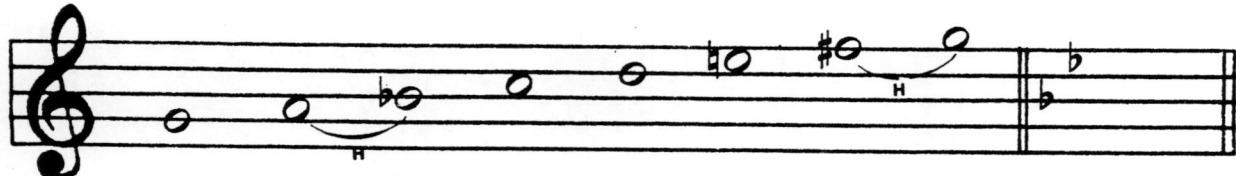

G MELODIC MINOR SCALE (descending)

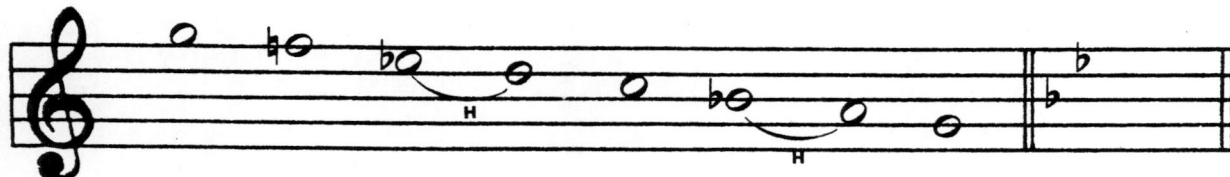

Draw the following minor scales. Mark the half-steps with slurs. Circle the step and a half interval in the harmonic form. Use accidentals and place the Key Signature after each scale.

d minor, harmonic form

d minor, melodic form (ascending and descending)

MEMORIZE THESE CHARTS.

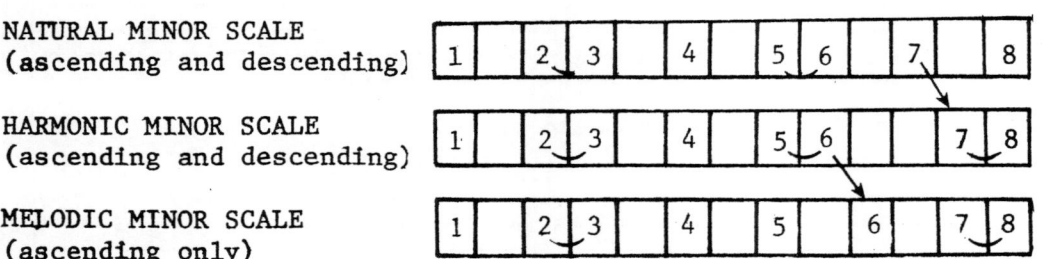

NATURAL MINOR SCALE
(ascending and descending)

HARMONIC MINOR SCALE
(ascending and descending)

7th
raised 1/2 step

MELODIC MINOR SCALE
(ascending only)

6th
raised 1/2 step

WORKSHEET

Draw the following scales. Use accidentals.

1. f minor, harmonic form   2. d minor, natural form

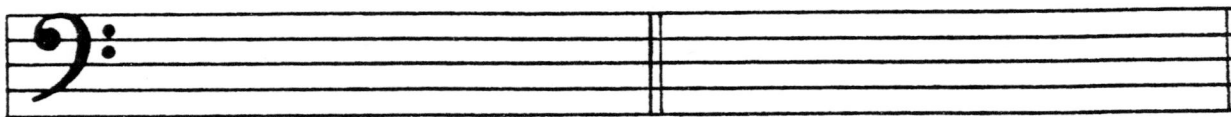

3. g minor, natural form   4. a minor, harmonic form

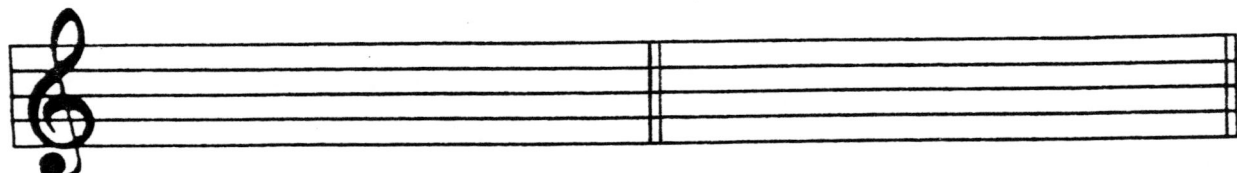

5. b♭ minor, melodic form (ascending and descending)

6. f♯ minor, harmonic form   7. a♭ minor, natural form

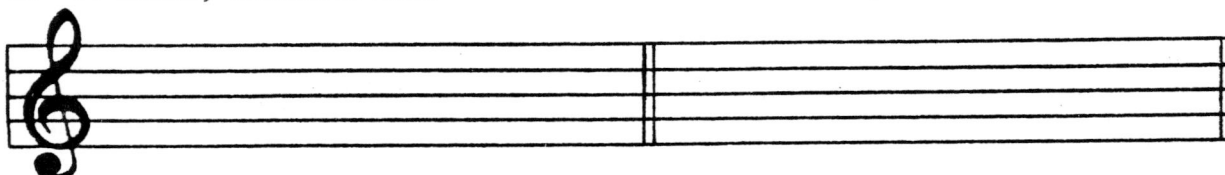

8. e minor, melodic form (ascending and descending)

9. e♭ minor, natural form   10. c♯ minor, harmonic form

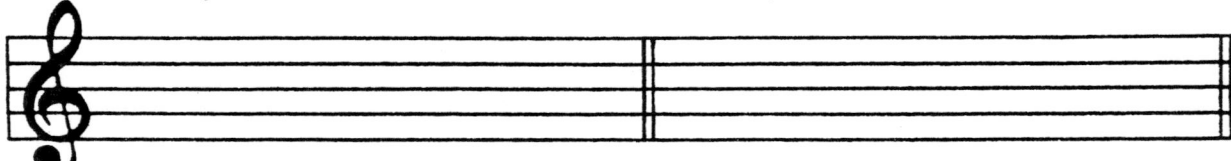

11. c minor, melodic form (ascending and descending)

12. b minor, melodic form (ascending and descending)

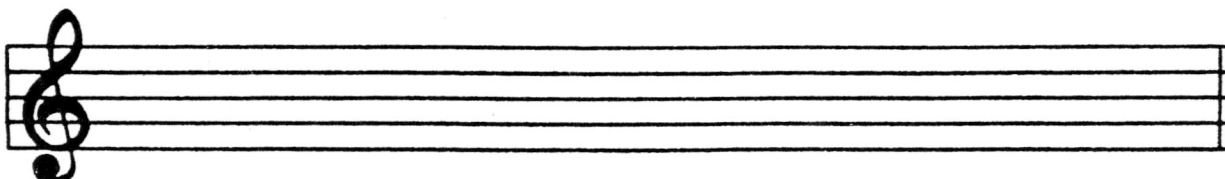

TRIADS OF THE HARMONIC MINOR SCALE

The triads built on tones of the harmonic minor scale will be either Major, minor, diminished or Augmented.

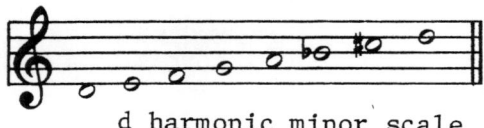

d harmonic minor scale

NOTATION OF MINOR SCALES: Major – large Roman numerals (V)
minor – small Roman numerals (iv)
diminished – small numerals with a circle (ii°)
Augmented – large numerals with a plus sign (III⁺)

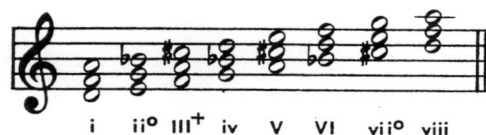

i   ii°   III⁺   iv   V   VI   vii°   viii

NOTE: The 7th degree of the d harmonic minor scale (c♯) appears in the triads built on the 3rd degree, 5th degree and 7th degree of the scale.

Draw the triads of the harmonic minor scales below. Use accidentals.
Label with Roman numerals.

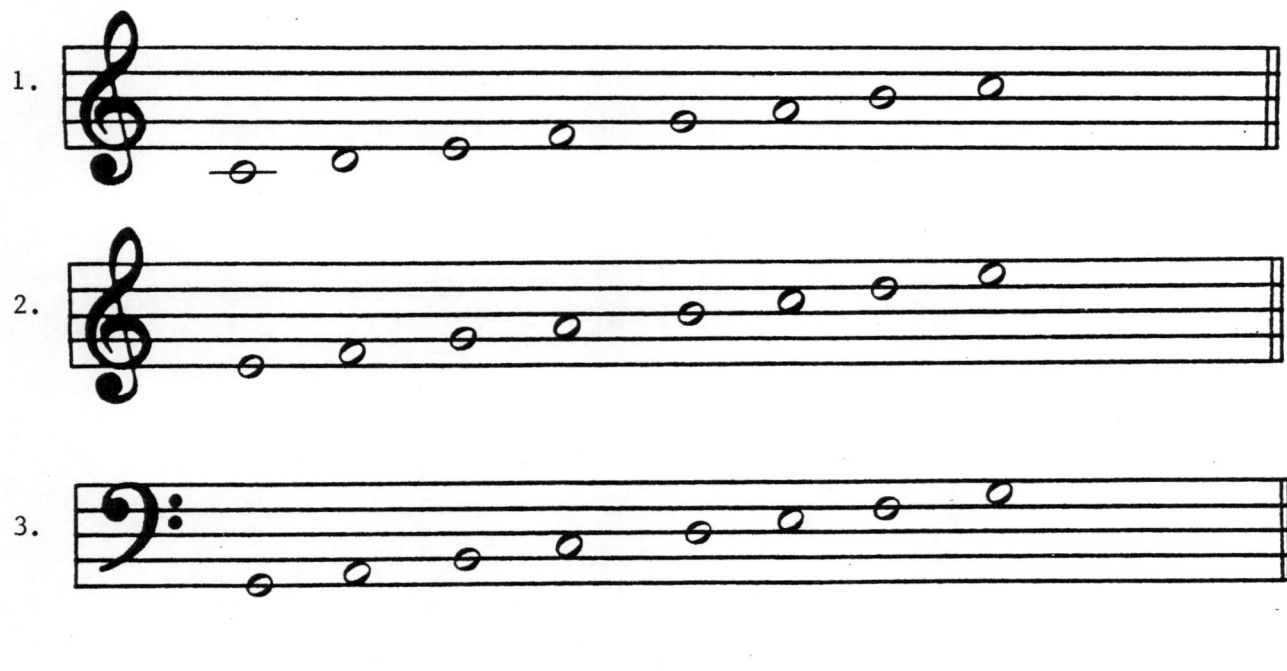

COMPOSITION ANALYSIS

1. a. Name the minor key. _____

   b. All three forms of the minor are used in this excerpt. Identify which form is used in each of the following measures.

   Measure 3. _____   5. _____   7. _____

   c. What accidentals indicate the melodic _____ _____ and the harmonic _____?

2. a. Name the minor key. _____

   b. What accidental indicates that the minor is in harmonic form? _____

   c. What is the texture? _____

3. a. Name the minor key. _____

   b. What accidental indicates that the minor is in harmonic form? _____

   c. Name the texture. _____

WORKSHEET

1. Major and minor scales with the same Key Signature are called _____.

2. Where is the interval of a step and a half found in the harmonic minor scale?

   _____

3. Complete the natural minor scale below. Use accidentals. Add the Key Signature after the scale.

4. The relative Major of the scale above is _____.

5. What tone is raised a half-step in a harmonic minor scale? _____

6. Complete the harmonic minor scale below. Use accidentals. Add the Key Signature after the scale.

7. The relative Major of the scale above is _____.

8. Draw triads on the harmonic minor scale tones below. Use accidentals.

9. What degree of the Major Scale is the tonic of its relative minor? _____

10. Draw the Major and relative minor tonics for these Key Signatures.

11. What are the six enharmonic Major keys? ___ ___, ___ ___, ___ ___

12. What are the six enharmonic minor keys? ___ ___, ___ ___, ___ ___

INTERVALS OF THE MAJOR AND HARMONIC MINOR SCALES

For intervals drawn above the tonic of a MAJOR SCALE, the 1st (prime), 4th, 5th and 8th (octave) are called PERFECT; all others are Major.

EXAMPLE:

In drawing intervals above the tonic of a HARMONIC MINOR SCALE, the 1st (prime), 4th, 5th and 8th (octave) are called PERFECT; the 3rd and 6th are MINOR; the 2nd and 7th are MAJOR.

EXAMPLE:

	MAJOR SCALE	HARMONIC MINOR SCALE
PERFECT INTERVALS	1st – 4th – 5th – 8th	1st – 4th – 5th – 8th
MAJOR INTERVALS	2nd – 3rd – 6th – 7th	2nd – 7th
MINOR INTERVALS		3rd – 6th

Draw intervals for the following scales. Use accidentals. Label with the quality and the number name.

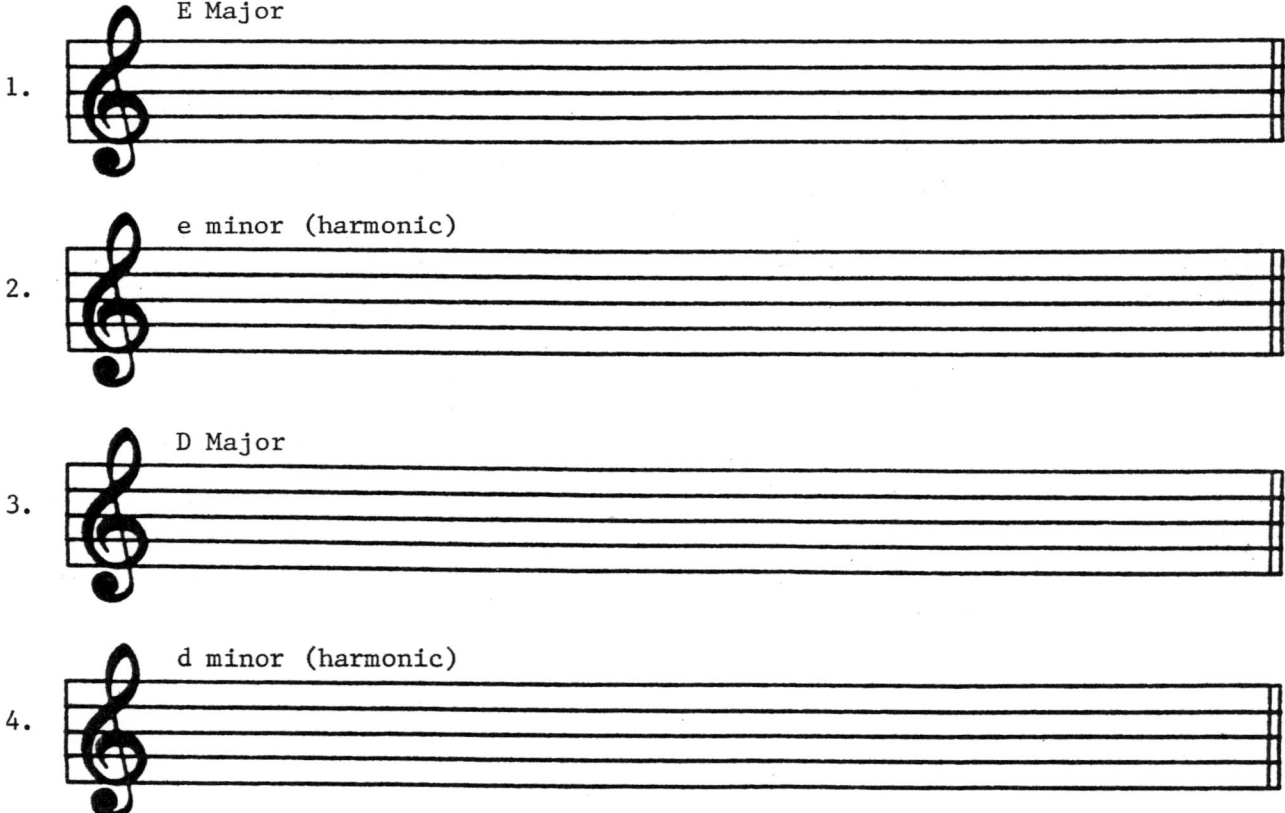

QUALITY OF INTERVALS IN COMPOSITIONS

MAJOR intervals are 2nds, 3rds, 6ths and 7ths above the tonic of the Major Scale.

PERFECT intervals are primes, fourths, fifths and octaves above the tonic of the Major Scale.

MINOR intervals are formed from the Major. Lower the upper tone one half-step.

DIMINISHED intervals are formed from the minor and Perfect intervals. Lower the upper tone one half-step.

AUGMENTED intervals are formed from the Major and Perfect intervals. Raise the upper tone one half-step.

To identify an interval in a composition, think of the lower tone as the tonic of a Major Scale and the upper tone as part of that scale. Then, determine whether the interval is Major or Perfect. If the interval is neither Major nor Perfect, use the above rules to find the quality.

EXAMPLE:

d5   A4   M2   d5   A4

1. Write the quality and number name of each circled harmonic interval in the excerpt below.

    Measure 1 _____, _____ 2 _____, _____ 4 _____, _____, _____
             5 _____

2. Write the quality and number name of each circled melodic interval in the excerpt below.

    Measure 1 _____, _____, _____ 5 _____, _____

CPT 5

INVERSION OF INTERVALS

All intervals may be inverted by changing the relative position of the two notes. Either <u>drop</u> the upper note an octave or <u>raise</u> the lower note an octave.

A SHORT-CUT TO INTERVAL INVERSION: The inversion of any interval can be found by subtracting the size of the interval from the number NINE. Memorize this rule.

EXAMPLE: An inverted 2nd becomes a 7th.   (9 − 2 = 7)

An inverted 4th becomes a 5th.   (9 − 4 = 5)

1. A 3rd becomes a _____ .   An octave becomes a _____ .

A 6th becomes a _____ .   A prime becomes an _____ .

A 5th becomes a _____ .   A 4th becomes a _____ .

A 2nd becomes a _____ .   A 7th becomes a _____ .

2. Invert the following intervals.   Label the inversion with number name.

5th ___   3rd ___   2nd ___   5th ___   6th ___   6th ___

7th ___   4th ___   6th ___   oct. ___   2nd ___   4th ___

3rd ___   6th ___   5th ___   oct. ___   2nd ___   7th ___

In the inversion of an interval, its <u>number name</u> is always changed. The combined numbers of the interval always add up to nine.

The quality of intervals will change in MAJOR, MINOR, DIMINISHED, and AUGMENTED interval inversions.

There is <u>no change</u> in classification of PERFECT INTERVALS when inverted.

A MAJOR interval inverts to a MINOR interval.   (M→m)
A MINOR interval inverts to a MAJOR interval.   (m→M)
An AUGMENTED interval inverts to a DIMINISHED interval.   (A→d)
A DIMINISHED interval inverts to an AUGMENTED interval.   (d→A)
A PERFECT interval inverts to another PERFECT interval.

1. Complete the following statements.

An Augmented 2nd inverts to a _____.

A Major 6th inverts to a _____.

A Perfect 5th inverts to a _____.

A Major 3rd inverts to a _____.

A Perfect Octave inverts to a _____.

A diminished 4th inverts to an _____.

A minor 7th inverts to a _____.

A Perfect Prime inverts to a _____.

An Augmented 3rd inverts to a _____.

2. Complete the harmonic intervals below. Draw the inversion of each interval and label with quality and number name. Use accidentals.

Example: M3   m6   P5 ___ m6 ___ M7 ___ d5 ___ A5 ___ A3 ___

M3 ___ P5 ___ m6 ___ M7 ___ P8 ___ A4 ___ M6 ___

CPT 5

COMPOUND INTERVALS

An interval of an octave or less is a simple interval. Any interval exceeding
an octave is compound. To make a simple interval compound, raise the top note
an octave or lower the bottom note an octave.

1. Draw simple intervals on each given note. Draw the compound interval by
    moving the upper note of the simple interval UP one octave.
    Label the compound intervals.

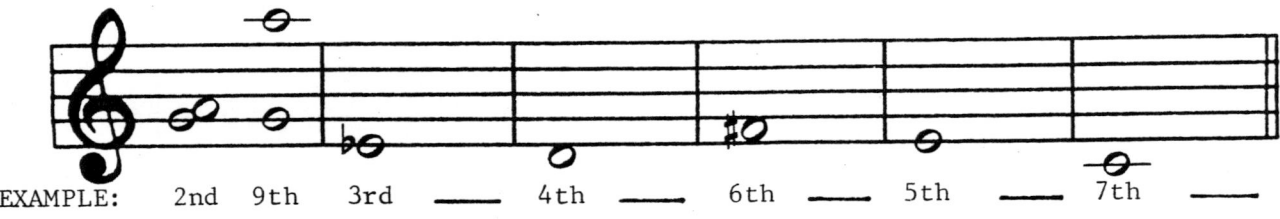

EXAMPLE: 2nd 9th   3rd ___   4th ___   6th ___   5th ___   7th ___

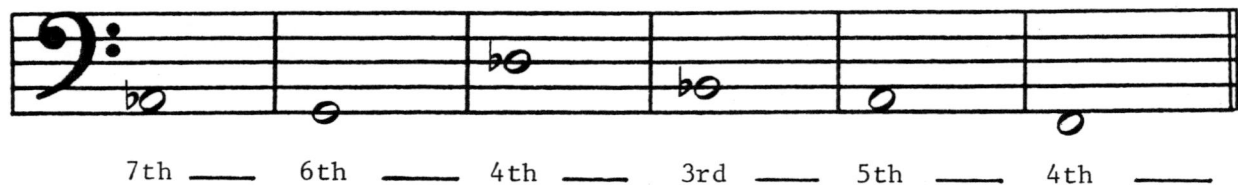

        7th ___   6th ___   4th ___   3rd ___   5th ___   4th ___

2. Draw simple intervals on each given note. Draw the compound interval by
    moving the lower note of the simple interval DOWN one octave.
    Label the compound intervals.

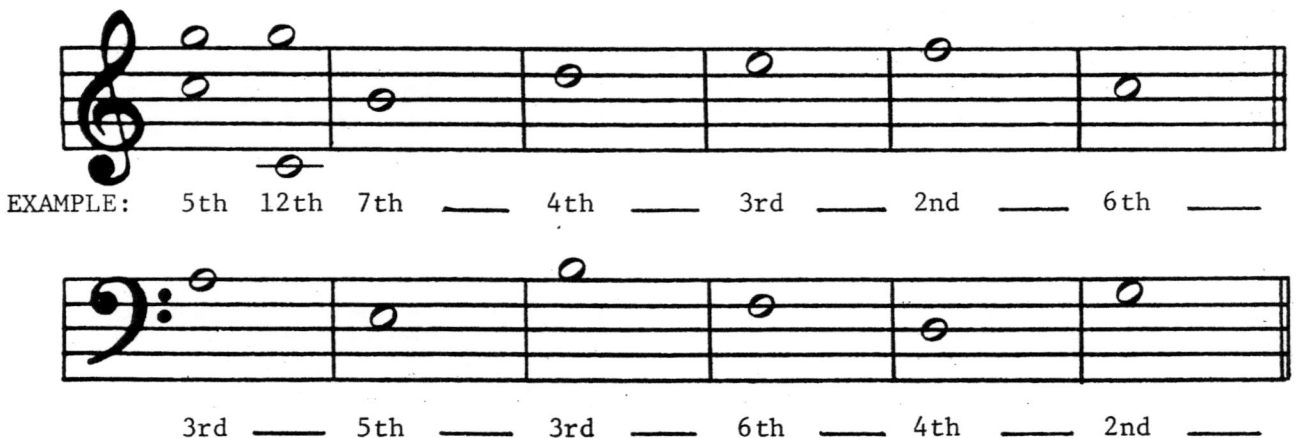

EXAMPLE: 5th 12th 7th ___   4th ___   3rd ___   2nd ___   6th ___

        3rd ___   5th ___   3rd ___   6th ___   4th ___   2nd ___

WORKSHEET

1. Write the quality of each third. Draw the inversions on the staff below.

2. How many different interval qualities are possible? _____

3. Label each interval with the quality and number name.
   Draw the inversions on the staff below.

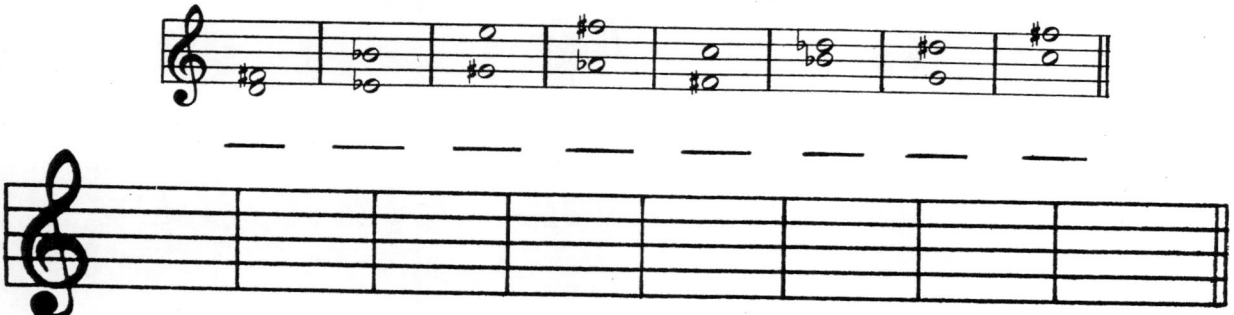

4. Write the quality and number name of each circled interval.

5. The excerpt below has both simple and compound intervals.
   Label each circled interval with an S or C.

CPT 5

COMPLEX METER, CHROMATIC SCALE, ORNAMENTATION

COMPLEX METER (Multimeter)

Music written with frequent changes of meter is common in the works of 20th Century composers.

EXAMPLE:

CHROMATIC SCALE

A scale consisting entirely of half-steps is called a chromatic scale.

EXAMPLE: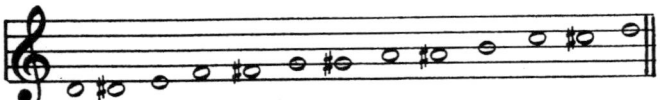

ORNAMENTATION

TRILL — The rapid alternation of a given note with the diatonic second above it. 𝆖 ∿

The beginning of a trill is often varied by the addition of a prefix. This is indicated by a modification of the ordinary sign.

⌣∿ from above

∿ from below

TURN — a group of four notes that turn around the principal note.
∾

MORDENT — The alternation of the written note with the note immediately below it. ∿

APPOGGIATURA — The *long appoggiatura* (♪♩) is played on the beat and usually takes half the value of the following note. The exact interpretation may vary in different periods of music.

                 written   played

EXAMPLE:    

— The *short appoggiatura* (♪♩) is played as a short note on the beat.
       written   played

EXAMPLE:    

TERMS

Match the following by placing the numbers on the lines.

TEMPO

1. Largo

2. Andante

3. Moderato

4. Grave

5. Presto

6. Alla Breve

TEXTURE

7. Chordal

8. Homophonic

9. Polyphonic

EXPRESSION

10. con Brio

11. Grazioso

12. Leggiero

13. Marcato

14. Misterioso

15. con Fuoco

16. Robusto

17. Tranquillo

COMPOSITIONAL TECHNIQUE and FORM

18. Repetition

19. Sequence

20. Imitation

21. Coda

_____ music consisting of a series of chords

_____ with fire

_____ motive is repeated in same voice

_____ gracefully, elegantly

_____ closing passage to emphasize finality

_____ walking speed

_____ mysteriously

_____ the slowest tempo marking

_____ with vigor and spirit

_____ moderate or medium

_____ light, nimble

_____ heavy, slow, solemn

_____ quietly, calmly

_____ very fast

_____ firmly and boldly

_____ music consisting of melodic line with chord accompaniment

_____ motive is repeated in different voice

_____ marked, with distinctness and emphasis

_____ tempo mark indicating ¢ or $\frac{2}{2}$ quick duple time

_____ music consisting of two or more melodies played simultaneously

_____ motive occurring in same voice but on different scale degrees

DOMINANT SEVENTH CHORDS

Dominant seventh chords were introduced in Level 4.

A dominant seventh chord in root position is often used with the root doubled and the fifth of the chord omitted. It can be written either on the Grand Staff or on a single staff.

There are several ways of writing the chord. The example shows two possible positions in the Key of C Major.

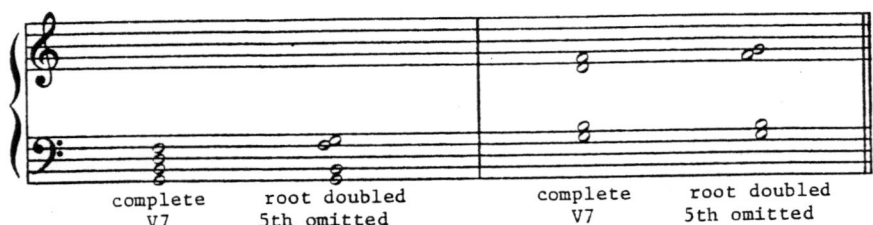

complete   root doubled   complete   root doubled
V7   5th omitted   V7   5th omitted

The third of the chord can also be omitted, although the omission of the fifth of the chord is more common.

This example shows two possible positions in the Key of C Major.

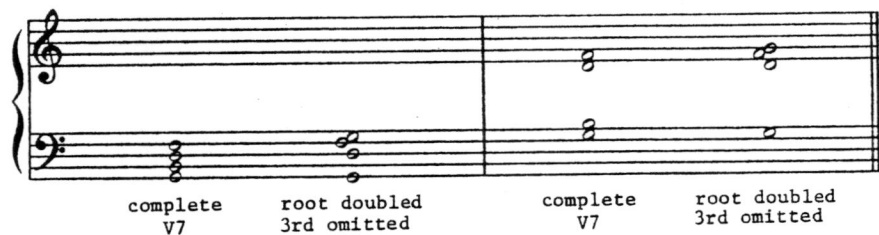

complete   root doubled   complete   root doubled
V7   3rd omitted   V7   3rd omitted

1. Draw two dominant seventh chords for each of the following keys on the Grand Staff. Draw one with all four notes and the other with the <u>fifth</u> omitted.

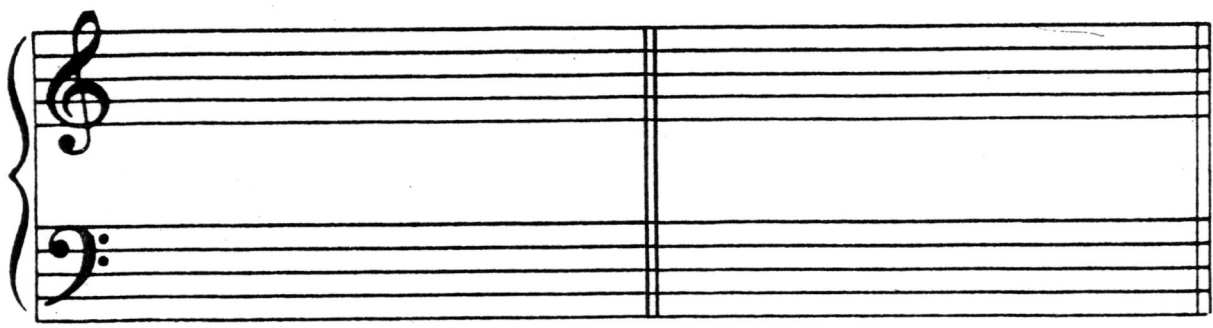

F Major   A Major

2. Draw two dominant seventh chords for each of the following keys on the Grand Staff. Draw one with all four notes and the other with the <u>third</u> omitted.

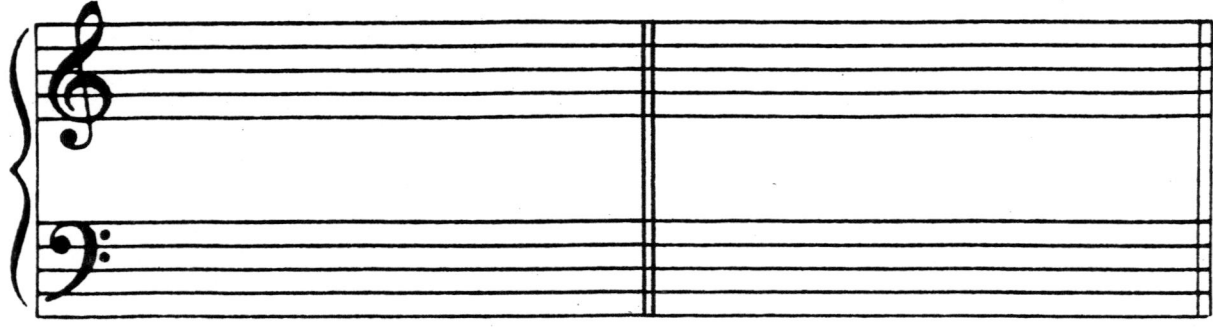

G Major   D Major

DOMINANT SEVENTH CHORDS
IN COMPOSITIONS

EXAMPLE:

1. Measures 1 and 2 of this excerpt are in the Key of a minor.
   The dominant seventh chord is in measure _____.
   Measures 3 - 6 are in the Key of C Major.
   The dominant seventh chord is in measure _____.

2. This excerpt is in the Key of F Major.
   The dominant seventh chord is in measure _____.
   Is the seventh chord written in melodic or
   harmonic form? _____

3. This excerpt is in the Key of g minor.
   The dominant seventh chord appears in
   measures 1 and 3.
   In which dominant seventh chord is the
   5th omitted? Measure _____
   Write the letter-name of the omitted
   5th. _____

CPT 5

COMPOSITION ANALYSIS

WALTZ IN B MINOR

CHOPIN

1. What is the texture of this excerpt? _____

2. What is the meter? _____ _____

3. Write the quality and number name of the circled melodic interval in measure 6. _____

4. Which measure has a complete dominant seventh chord in root position? _____

5. Write the quality and number name of the circled melodic interval in measure 14. _____

6. Write the quality and number name of the circled harmonic interval in measure 15. _____

7. Write the quality and number name of the circled harmonic interval in measure 16. _____

KEY CHANGES THROUGH MODULATION

MODULATION means to pass from one key to another with the use of accidentals and without a change in Key Signature.

A composition written in the Key of G Major has an F♯ in the Key Signature, and the chord structure shows a positive identity with the Key of G Major.

If there is a repeated use of other accidentals, it is possible that the composition has modulated to another key. This may be a passing modulation, one in which the key is quickly regained, or a final modulation, one in which the new key remains.

If a composition is written in the Key of G Major (F♯) and there is a consistent use of the accidental C♯, the piece could be modulating to the Key of D Major (F♯ and C♯).

Below is an excerpt from an ETUDE by Bertini.

1. Name the accidental which indicates a modulation to another key. _____

2. What is the beginning key? _____   To what key does the piece modulate? _____

3. The dominant seventh of the new key appears in measure 9. What is the letter-name of the seventh chord? _____   What is the inversion? _____
   (Remember to look in the treble melody for the missing note of the chord.)

4. In the beginning key, write the scale degree and figured bass symbol of each underscored chord.   Measure 1. _____ _____   3. _____ _____

5. In the new key, write the scale degree and figured bass symbol of each underscored chord.   Measure 9. _____ _____   11. _____ _____   13. _____ _____
   14. _____ _____

CADENCES

Cadences are formed from the triads of a scale. In the earlier levels of this series, cadences were written on a single staff to enable the student to clearly see their construction. However, in a composition the cadence is usually formed on the Grand Staff, often with a dominant seventh chord. The examples below show the usual arrangement of notes with the root of the tonic doubled. Tones common to both chords are usually kept in the same voice.

EXAMPLES:

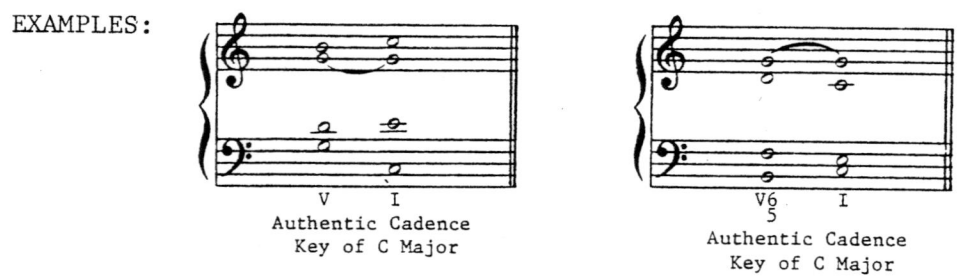

1. Draw an Authentic Cadence in the following keys on the Grand Staff below. Use accidentals. Connect each common tone with a slur.

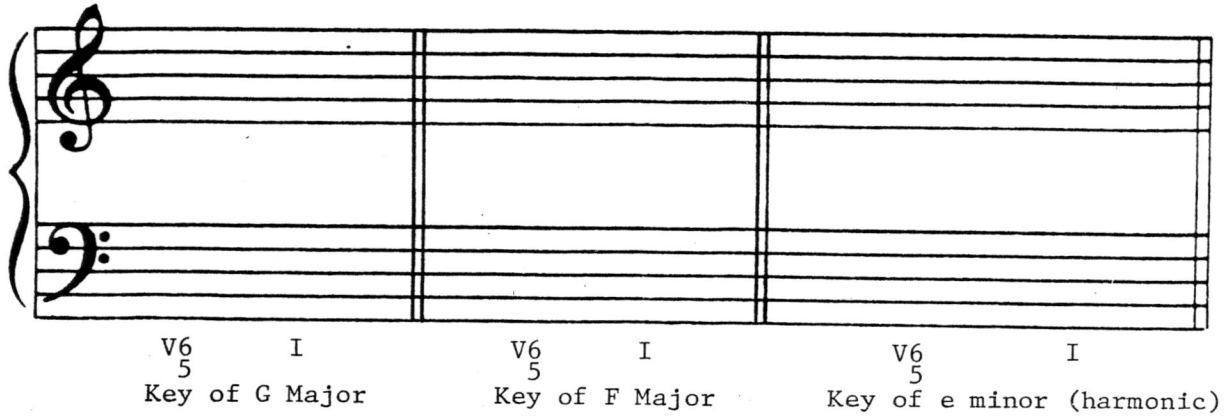

Cadences are found written on the Grand Staff in various positions. In the examples the root of the tonic chord is used in the bass and soprano voices to give a more final sound.

EXAMPLES:

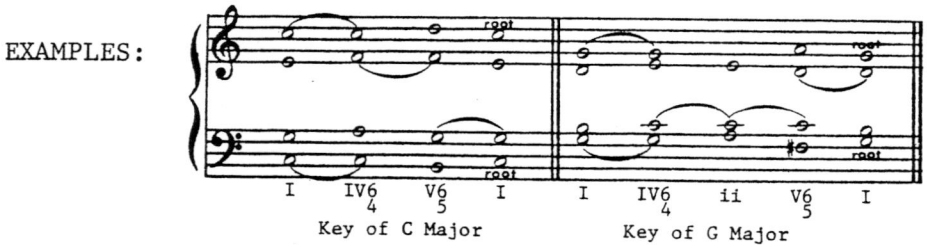

2. Draw the chord progressions on the Grand Staff below. Use accidentals. Connect each common tone with a slur.

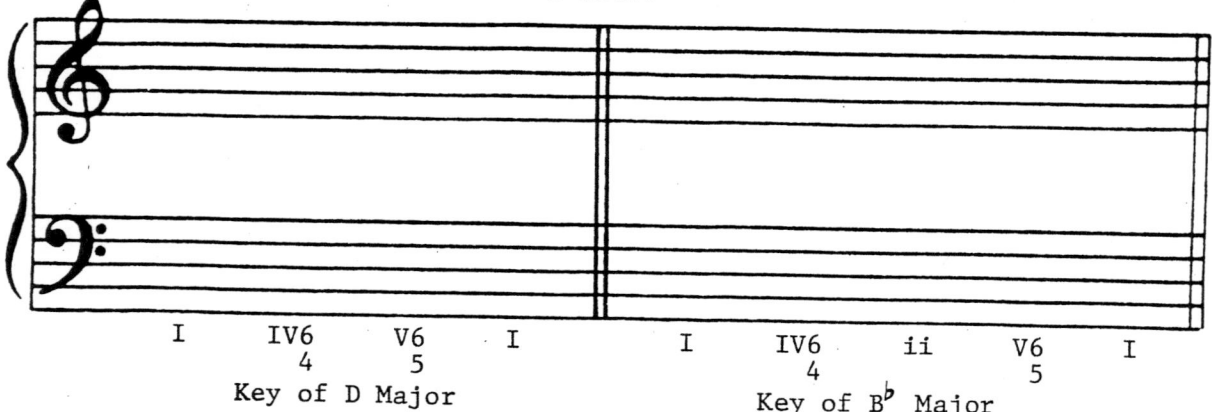

3. Label the underscored chord progressions with Roman numerals and
figured bass symbols.

RONDO in F

RONDO FORM

Rondo form is an extension of the ternary form. Ternary form has two themes: the first theme is repeated upon the completion of the second theme (A B A). Rondo form has three or more themes. The first theme is repeated at the conclusion of each new theme (A B A C A B A). See the example on page 26.

COMPOSITION ANALYSIS

Answer the following questions on the Rondo by Wolfgang Amadeus Mozart.

1. What is the key of the A section? _____

2. The meter is _____ . _____ .

3. Name the underscored cadence in measures 15 and 16. _____

4. There is a key change in the B section. The composition modulates to a minor key. Name the minor key. _____

5. In what way is this minor key related to the key in the A section? _____

    _____

6. The passage from measure 26 to 30 is in what form of this minor key? _____

7. What accidental indicates this minor form? _____

8. Name the ornament in measure 29. _____

9. In section C the composition again modulates to a minor key. Name the minor key.

    _____

10. In what way is the minor key in section C related to the original key in section A?

    _____

TRANSPOSITION

To change a composition to another key is called <u>TRANSPOSITION</u>.

One way of transposing music is by scale degrees.

<u>SCALE DEGREES</u> (scale numbers)

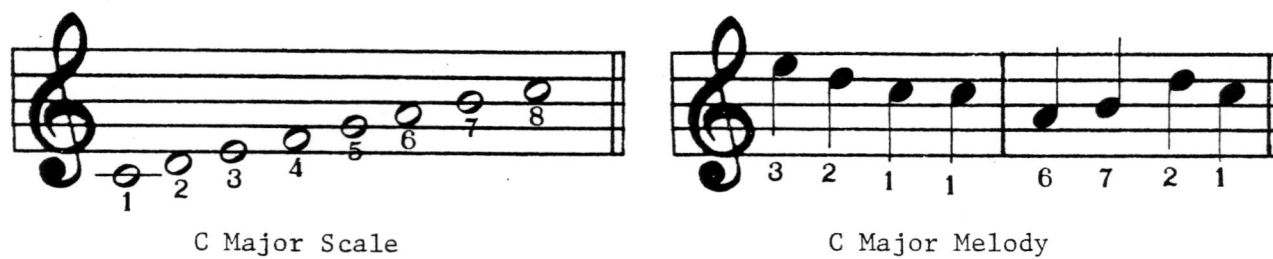

C Major Scale   C Major Melody

The above melody is written in the Key of C Major. The notes are numbered by scale degrees. To transpose this melody into the Key of E♭ Major, use the same scale degrees of the E♭ Major Scale.

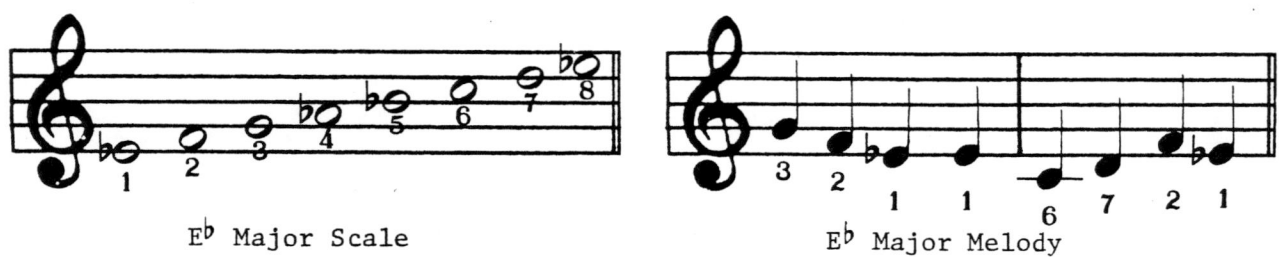

E♭ Major Scale   E♭ Major Melody

The melody below is written in the Key of G Major.
Transpose the melody into the following keys.

MODES

(Introduced in Level 4)

Early modes were written on white keys only. However, in compositions today, modes may be written in other keys with the use of accidentals.

The Ionian mode has the same arrangement of whole steps and half-steps as the Major Scales. The arrangement of whole steps and half-steps in the Aeolian mode is the same as that in the natural minor scales.

Any mode may be recognized by the arrangement of whole steps and half-steps.

Draw the following modal scales and transpose them. Mark the half-steps.

EXAMPLE:

AEOLIAN MODE (original)   (transposed)

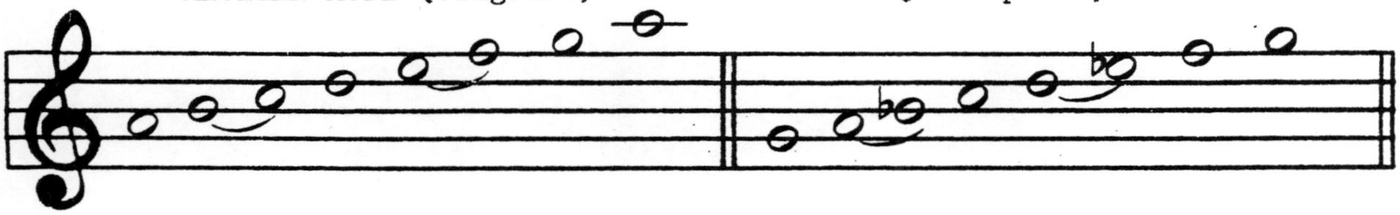

DORIAN MODE

PHRYGIAN MODE

LYDIAN MODE

MIXOLYDIAN MODE

SONATA-ALLEGRO FORM

The SONATA-ALLEGRO FORM, sometimes called the first movement form, is very important in the Classical sonata.

The sonata-allegro form has three divisions:

I. EXPOSITION

    1. Principal Theme (P.T.) has a clearly defined Major or minor tonality.

    2. Episode leads to the *Secondary Theme*.

    3. Secondary Theme (S.T.) is written in the relative Major key when the P.T. is minor, or in the dominant Major key when the P.T. is Major. (This is the usual form; exceptions do occur.)

II. DEVELOPMENT

    The themes established in the exposition are developed through key changes, rhythmic changes, or a different treatment of motives.

III. RECAPITULATION

    1. Principal Theme is in the original key.

    2. Modulating Passage leads to the *Secondary Theme*.

    3. Secondary Theme is in the same key as the Principal Theme.

    4. Closing Theme (C.T.) is in the same key as the Principal Theme.

Often the sonata-allegro form is preceded by an introduction, and ended with a coda.

THE SONATA

A SONATA is a composition made up of two or more movements for a solo instrument. These movements differ in rhythm, tempo, or form.

In a sonata with three movements, there is usually (1) a fast movement, (2) a slow movement, usually quiet in style, and (3) a finale in quicker tempo, often in rondo form.

If there is a fourth movement, it may be found after the slow movement in the form of a scherzo and/or minuet.

If there are only two movements in a sonata, one will be in sonata-allegro form, and one will be in any of the other forms.

COMPOSERS OF THE SONATA

Baroque composers Johann Sebastian Bach, George Frideric Handel, and Domenico Scarlatti were all born in the year 1685.

Of these three composers, Scarlatti is best known for his sonatas. He wrote 550 one-movement sonatas, all in binary form, not sonata-allegro form.

The writing for the clavier and the pianoforte took new forms during the time approaching the Classical period of music writing. Three of J. S. Bach's sons—Wilhelm Friedemann Bach (1710-84), Karl Philipp Emanuel Bach (1714-88), Johann Christian Bach (1735-82)—contributed to the expansion of the sonata.

Wm. F. Bach added new harmonies and strong themes to his sonatas.

K. P. E. Bach's sonatas usually have an allegro, an adagio, and a rondo movement. His most important work is found in his sonatas for the clavier. He was instrumental in developing the sonata-allegro form and the Classical sonata.

J. Ch. Bach developed a very melodic style in his sonatas, and his first movements contain two complete subjects. He used the pianoforte more than the harpsichord—perhaps the first musician to do so.

Joseph Haydn (1732-1809) wrote fifty-two piano sonatas. He inherited all the sonata structure and the homophonic texture of writing from K. P. E. Bach, and developed a more expansive form. Some historians regard Haydn as a direct link in the development of the sonata from K. P. E. Bach to Beethoven.

Wolfgang Amadeus Mozart (1756-91) wrote and performed his clavier works for the harpsichord. Although he used the pianoforte for his later concerts, his technique and style did not change.

Ludwig van Beethoven (1770-1827) wrote thirty-two piano sonatas. He enlarged on the Classical form and perfected it. He introduced new ideas of development and a wide range of change in mood and color.

THE SONATINA

The SONATINA plays an important part in the study of piano. Sonatinas are helpful in the development of technique, musicianship, and in the understanding of the larger and more complex sonata.

SONATINAS as "small sonatas" usually have three movements, although many are written in two. One of the movements may have the sonata-allegro form, but often the development section is replaced by a short interlude or "bridge" so that the exposition is followed by the recapitulation.

HISTORICAL CONSIDERATIONS

BAROQUE

Performers were expected to add notes to those the composer had written. Ornaments originated in improvisation in early music. Later they were partially or entirely written out, or indicated by special signs. Ornaments were added to enhance and sustain the melody and make it more interesting.

Keyboard music was written for the harpsichord, clavichord or organ. The sound on the harpsichord and organ could not be varied or controlled by means of finger touch. Different degrees of loudness were possible only by special hand stops. Consequently the dynamic levels were kept the same or changed only by using the hand stops, thus creating terraced dynamics. To interpret early Baroque music on the piano of today, the pianist often uses terraced dynamics to create the effect used on the early keyboard instruments.

This is an example of polyphonic texture which was often used in Baroque music.

CLASSICAL

Improvisation was continued during the Classical period by Clementi, Mozart, and others. This period introduced new musical forms and concepts. The sonata form, minuet and trio, and rondo were used; binary, ternary, and theme-and-variations were adopted to the Classical style. Contrasts between sections and within sections of these forms were expressed by using two keys and/or abrupt melodic shifts from Major to minor. Melodies had a singing quality. Homophonic texture predominates, although many compositions combine all three types of texture.

Alberti bass was developed during the Classical period by the Italian composer, Domenico Alberti (1710-40). This device consists of broken left-hand chords, which tend to set off the melody to great advantage and provide a feeling of forward motion.

This is an example of Alberti bass.

ROMANTIC

The Romantic period brought about an expansion of melodic, dramatic, and rhythmic conceptions. Romantic music was inspired by moods, ideas, stories, scenes or even dramatic plays. Harmonies were more colorful. Unusual chord progressions were used. Melody lines were more lyrical. Rhythmic patterns were also more complicated using the "two against three" and "three against four" arrangements of notes. With the use of chromatic harmonies, complex chords, and freer use of non-harmonic tones, the tonality is more difficult to identify.

This is an example of the "two against three" arrangement.

MODERN (CONTEMPORARY)

Much of the music of the Twentieth Century introduces a rejection of definite tonality. Arnold Schönberg completely eliminated the tonal center by using the twelve tones of the chromatic scale with each tone having equal importance. Atonality prevails in most compositions written in this manner.

Bitonality is also widely used. A composition written with one tonality in the right hand played against another tonality in the left hand creates new tonal effects.

Quartal harmony is another concept used in Contemporary music. Harmonic structure is based upon the interval of the fourth, as opposed to the traditional system based on the third. For example, the fourth chord consisting of C-F-B♭ would take the place of the C-E-G triad.

This is an example of bitonality with c minor in the right hand and c phrygian in the left hand.

BAROQUE

This excerpt is from a Sonata by Scarlatti (1685-1757).

COMPOSITION ANALYSIS

1. In what period of music was this piece written? _____

2. Circle the names of the other composers who lived during this period.

   Chopin   J. S. Bach   Mozart   Handel

3. Name two keyboard instruments of this period.

   _____   _____

4. What is the meter of this piece? _____

5. This sonata is written in a minor key. Name the key. _____

6. What form of the minor is used in the first three measures? _____

7. What accidental indicates this form? _____

8. What is the texture of this piece? _____

9. Name the ornaments in measure 3. _____

10. Are these ornaments played before or on the beat in this period of music?

    _____

11. Write the quality and number name of each harmonic interval in measure 4.

    _____   _____

12. Circle the term that applies to measures 6 and 7.

    Sequence   Repetition

13. A modulation begins in measure 7. Write the name of the new key and list
    the accidentals that indicate this change.

    _____   _____   _____

14. What measure is identical to measure 8? _____

15. List the quality and number name of each melodic interval in the Treble Clef
    of measure 15.

    _____, _____, _____, _____, _____, _____,

    _____, _____, _____, _____, _____

CPT 5

CLASSICAL

Allegro

COMPOSITION ANALYSIS

This excerpt is from Sonatina Op. 55 No. 1 by Kuhlau (1786-1832).

1. The sonata-allegro form has three distinct divisions. List each one.

   _____   _____   _____

2. Define sonatina. _____

3. What may replace the development section of the sonata-allegro form in a sonatina?

   _____

4. In what period of music was this sonatina written? _____

5. What is the tonality of this sonatina? _____

6. What is the meter? _____

7. What is the texture? _____

8. Circle the term that applies to measures 1 and 2.

   Imitation   Sequence   Repetition

9. What repeated accidental indicates a modulation? _____

10. To what key does the excerpt modulate? _____

11. Name the melodic seventh chord in measure 5. _____

12. Write the quality and number name of each circled interval.

   Measure 1. _____ 2. _____ 10. _____

   11. _____ 12. _____ 14. _____

13. The bass in measures 9-12 is called _____.

14. Name the Major Scale found in measures 15 and 16. _____

15. Circle the term that applies to the bracketed passage in measures 13 and 14.

   Imitation   Sequence   Repetition

16. Name the underscored cadence in measures 19 and 20. _____

ROMANTIC

COMPOSITION ANALYSIS

This excerpt is from Children's Pieces Op. 72 by Mendelssohn (1809-47).

1. The first antecedent phrase is found in measures _____, _____, _____, _____.

2. The first consequent phrase is found in measures _____, _____, _____, _____.

3. Write the Roman numeral and figured bass symbol for the circled triad in measure 4. _____ _____

4. Write the letter-name and figured bass symbol for the circled dominant seventh chord in measure 7. _____ _____

5. Name the underscored cadence in measures 7 and 8. _____

6. List the quality and number name of each harmonic interval in the Treble Clef in measure 9.

   _____, _____, _____, _____, _____

7. Name the accidental that indicates a modulation to another key. _____

8. To what key does the piece modulate? _____

9. In what measure does it return to the original key? _____

10. Name the accidental that indicates this change. _____

11. Name the circled scale in measures 27-29. _____

12. What is the meaning of the dynamic mark in measure 29? _____

13. List the size and quality of each harmonic interval in the Treble Clef in measure 34.

    _____, _____, _____

14. Give the name and meaning of the sign above the last measure.

    _____   _____

15. In what period of music was this piece written? _____

CONTEMPORARY - COMPOSITION ANALYSIS

This is an excerpt from a piece by Kabalevsky.

1a.   What is the meter? _____   b.   What does leggiero mean? _____

  c.   Name the term that describes the circled passage in measure 2. _____

This is an excerpt from a piece by Villa-Lobos.

2a.   What is the meter? _____
  b.   Give the Italian name for this Time Signature. _____
  c.   What is the key? _____
  d.   What does the e♮ in the Bass Clef indicate?
  _____

This is an excerpt from a piece by Bartók.

3a.   What is the meter? _____

  b.   Name the three Time Signatures used.   _____   _____   _____

<u>TEST</u>

1. Draw the Key Signature on the Grand Staff for each Major key below.
   Draw the Major key-tone and the relative minor key-tone on each staff.

2. Write the name of the relative minor.

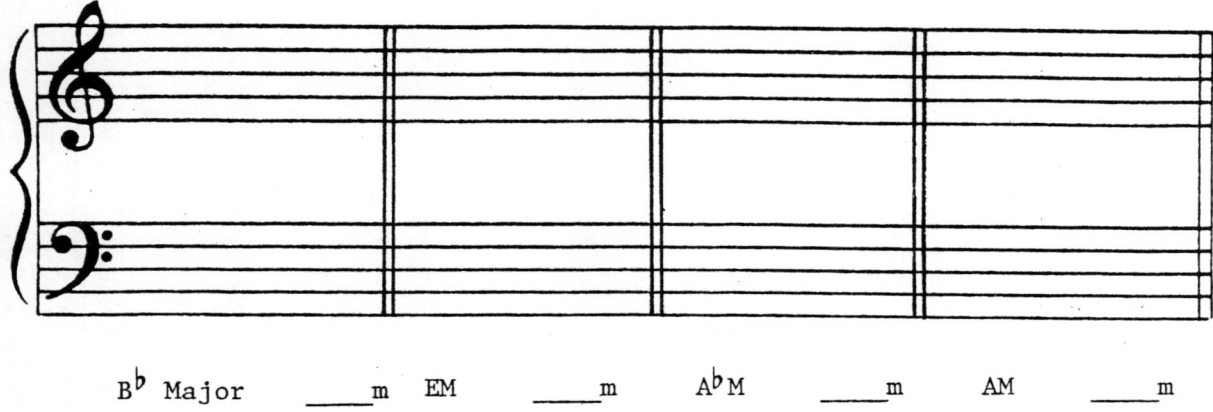

B♭ Major _____m   EM _____m   A♭M _____m   AM _____m

3. Complete the charts for the Major and the three forms of the ascending minor
   scales. Use scale numbers. (Each square represents a half-step.)

Major Scale: 1
Natural Minor: 1
Harmonic Minor: 1
Melodic Minor: 1

4. What change is made in the descending melodic minor scale?

_____

5. Draw the following scales one ascending octave. Draw and label the three
   Primary triads for each one. Use accidentals.

D Major

c natural minor

c harmonic minor

c melodic minor (ascending)

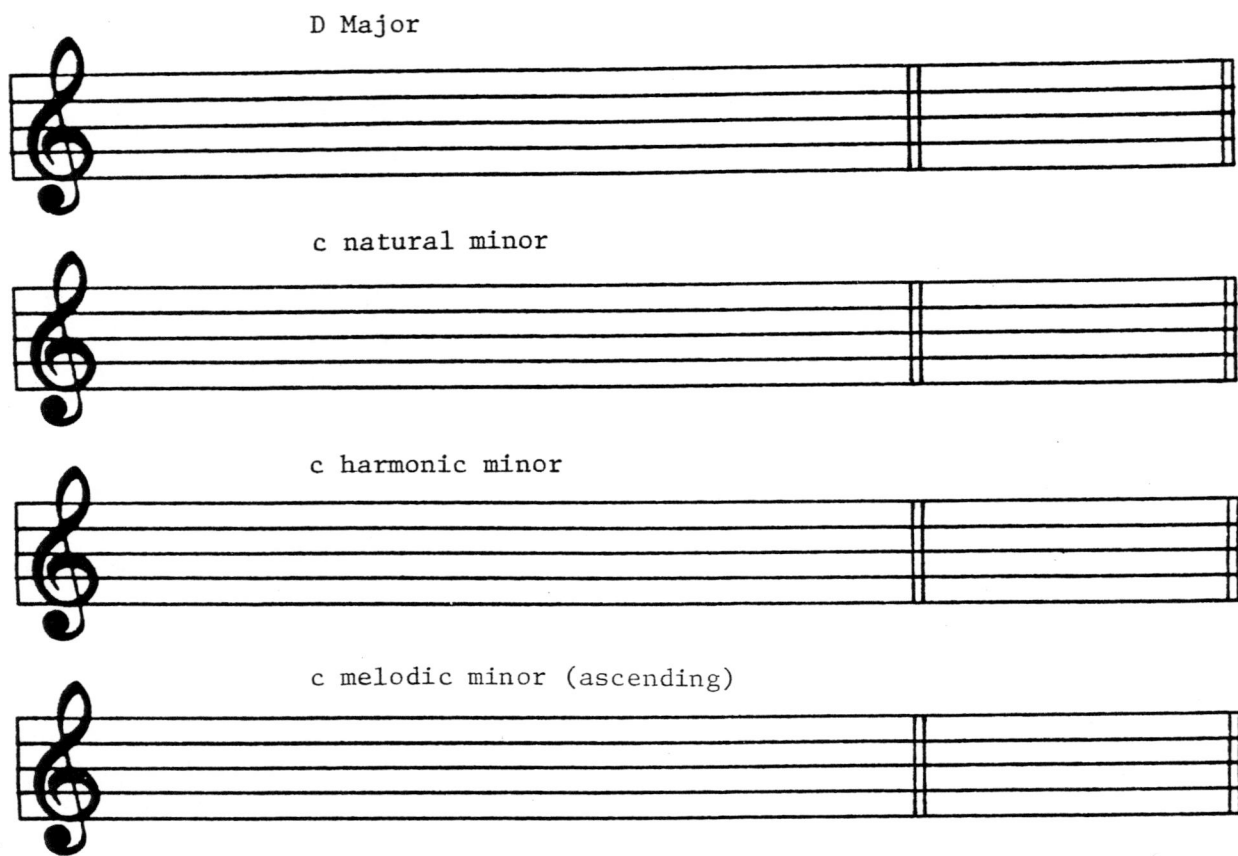

6. Draw intervals for the following ascending scales. Label size and quality. Draw
   the Key Signature after each scale.

d minor, natural form

g minor, harmonic form

e minor, melodic form (ascending)

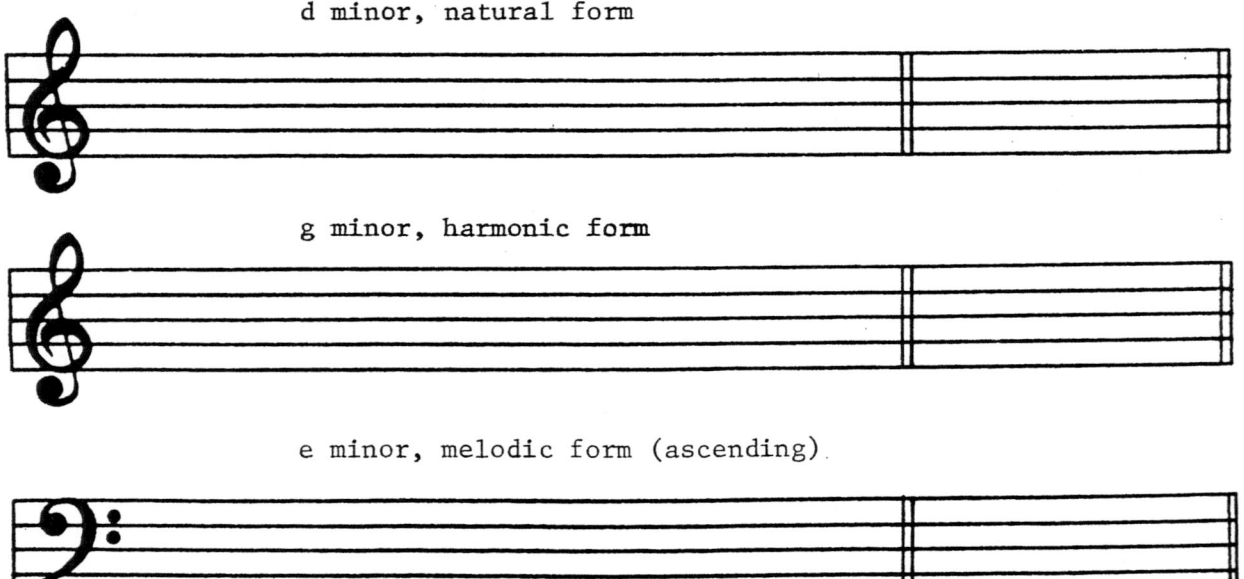

7. Draw the triads of the harmonic minor scales below. Use accidentals.
   Draw the Key Signature after each scale.

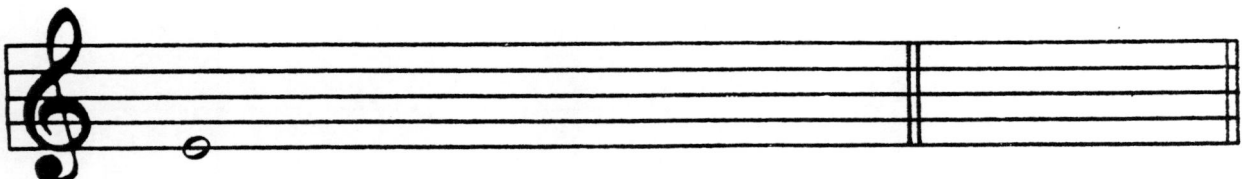

8. a. What is the scale passage in the Treble Clef called? _____

    b. List the quality and number name of each circled interval.

        _____   _____   _____

    c. What is the position of the circled seventh chord? _____

9. a. Name the minor key. _____

    b. What form of the minor is used? _____

    c. Name the accidentals that indicate this form. _____   _____

    d. What is the texture? _____

10. Complete the following statements.

A Major 6th inverts to a _____.

A Perfect octave inverts to a _____.

A diminished 4th inverts to an _____.

A minor 2nd inverts to a _____.

An Augmented 5th inverts to a _____.

11. Transpose this melody into the Key of E Major.

12. The dominant seventh chord (V7) is built on the _____ degree of a diatonic scale.

13. Draw V7 chords in root position and inversions in the keys below. Label with figured bass symbols.

14. Draw simple and compound intervals on the notes below.

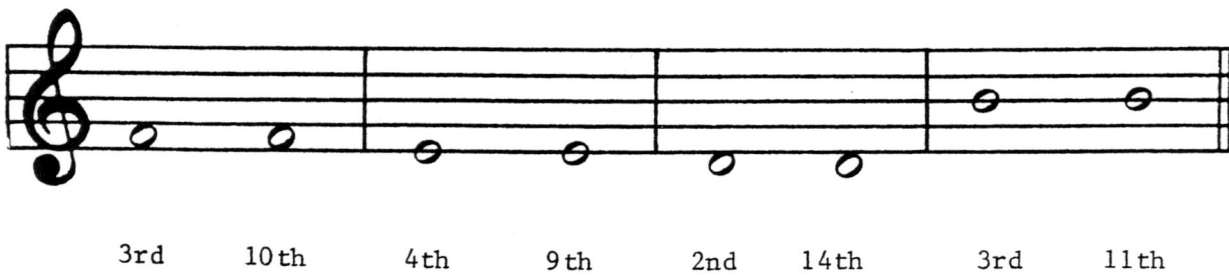

3rd   10th   4th   9th   2nd   14th   3rd   11th

15. a. This excerpt is written in E♭ Major. The accidentals indicate a modulation to what key?

    _____

    b. Name the underscored cadence. _____

16. Circle the form that identifies A B A C A B A.

    Ternary   Binary   Rondo

17. Name the following modes.

    _____   _____

18. Name the three divisions of sonata-allegro form.

    _____   _____   _____

19. Name two composers who are well known for their Classical sonatas.

    _____   _____

20. Circle the term that describes a composition written with two different tonalities.

    Atonality   Bitonality

21. Define the following terms.

    con fuoco   _____

    grave   _____

    largo   _____

    marcato   _____

    dolce   _____

COMPOSITION ANALYSIS

This excerpt is from Sonatina Op. 55 No. 4 by Kuhlau.

1. What is the key of this movement? _____

2. What is the meter? _____

3. What is the texture of the first eight measures? _____

4. Name the underscored cadence in measures 7 and 8. _____

5. What is the texture of measures 9-27? _____

6. List the quality and number name of each circled interval.

    Measure 1. _____   2. _____   3. _____   4. _____ _____   5. _____ _____

    6. _____ _____   7. _____   9. _____   12. _____   16. _____ _____

    18. _____   19. _____   21. _____   22. _____   23. _____   25. _____

7. What measures form the coda? _____

Andantino con espressione.